GEOLOGY GENIUS
CRYSTALS

by Rebecca Pettiford

Ideas for Parents and Teachers

Pogo Books let children practice reading informational text while introducing them to nonfiction features such as headings, labels, sidebars, maps, and diagrams, as well as a table of contents, glossary, and index.

Carefully leveled text with a strong photo match offers early fluent readers the support they need to succeed.

Before Reading

- "Walk" through the book and point out the various nonfiction features. Ask the student what purpose each feature serves.
- Look at the glossary together. Read and discuss the words.

Read the Book

- Have the child read the book independently.
- Invite him or her to list questions that arise from reading.

After Reading

- Discuss the child's questions. Talk about how he or she might find answers to those questions.
- Prompt the child to think more. Ask: Have you ever broken open a geode? Did you know how geodes formed before you read this book?

Pogo Books are published by Jump!
5357 Penn Avenue South
Minneapolis, MN 55419
www.jumplibrary.com

Library of Congress Cataloging-in-Publication Data

Names: Pettiford, Rebecca, author.
Title: Crystals: geology genius / by Rebecca Pettiford.
Description: Minneapolis, MN: Jump!, Inc., [2018]
Series: Geology genius | "Pogo Books are published by Jump!" | Audience: Ages 7-10. | Includes bibliographical references and index.
Identifiers: LCCN 2017044912
ISBN 9781624968242 (hardcover: alk. paper)
ISBN 9781624968259 (pbk.)
ISBN 9781624968266 (ebook)
Subjects: LCSH: Crystals–Juvenile literature. Crystallography–Juvenile literature.
Classification: LCC QD921 .P4727 2018 | DDC 548–dc23
LC record available at https://lccn.loc.gov/2017044912

Editor: Kristine Spanier
Book Designer: Michelle Sonnek
Content Consultant: Sandra Feher, M.S.G.E.

Photo Credits: All photos by Shutterstock except: Scott Camazine/Alamy, 8-9; Carsten Peter/Speleoresearch & Films/Getty, 12-13; DEA/C. DANI/I.JESKE/Getty, 14-15; Andy Sutton/Alamy, 17; Matteo Chinellato - ChinellatoPhoto/Getty, 18-19; pncphotos/Dreamstime, 20-21.

Printed in the United States of America at Corporate Graphics in North Mankato, Minnesota.

TABLE OF CONTENTS

CHAPTER 1

WHAT ARE CRYSTALS?

What do diamonds and snowflakes have in common? They are crystals! Crystals are solid **matter**. Matter is made of two things. **Atoms**. And **molecules**. These are too small to see with your eyes.

Crystals are everywhere. They are in **minerals**. Minerals are in rocks. The sand on a beach is many broken mineral crystals.

Crystals have sharp corners. They have a regular pattern of flat surfaces. As the crystal grows, the pattern of the shape grows. This helps to identify what it is made of. All salt crystals look like cubes. **Quartz** crystals look like hexagons.

salt crystal

TAKE A LOOK!

Crystals can be divided into seven general patterns. Different crystals can share the same one. Compare them.

cubic
examples:
gold, salt

triclinic
examples:
albite, rhodonite

tetragonal
examples:
chalcopyrite, zircon

hexagonal
examples:
calcite, quartz

orthorhombic
examples:
aragonite, sulfur

trigonal
examples:
amethyst, hematite

monoclinic
examples:
mica, selenite

rhodonite

gold

sulfur

agate

Many gemstones are crystals.
Metals like gold and silver
are crystals, too.

DID YOU KNOW?

Crystals are in things we use every day. They are in **compounds** like salt. Quartz crystals are in clocks. Glass is not a crystal. Why not? Its molecules are not arranged in a repeating pattern.

CHAPTER 2

HOW CRYSTALS FORM

Crystals form when a liquid changes to a solid. **Magma** is melted rock. It cools. Crystals form.

Water dissolves minerals. It carries those minerals away. They enter **cavities** in other rocks. The water cools. It **evaporates**. The cavities slowly fill with crystals. These are known as geodes.

◀ · · · · · geode

Cave of the Crystals is in Mexico. It has some of the largest crystals in the world. Many are 36 feet (11 meters) high. They have been growing for more than 500,000 years. How do they grow?

The cave has water in it. **Gypsum** is in the water. Magma under the cave heats the water. It cools. It evaporates. The gypsum leaves behind **selenite** crystals.

selenite crystal

The Reed Flute Cave is in China. It was once filled with water. **Calcite** crystals formed from limestone in the water. Now they are lit with colored lights.

DID YOU KNOW?

This cave has had visitors for more than 1,000 years. How do we know? They left marks on the walls. Now this is against the rules.

CHAPTER 3

HUNTING FOR CRYSTALS

Where can we find crystals? The areas around **hot springs** are good places. The heated water pushes minerals to the surface. The water evaporates. It leaves crystals behind.

aragonite

agate

amethyst

Ribbons of white quartz can be found near **fault** lines.

white quartz

Hematite crystals can form inside a **volcano**. Volcanic activity sends them to the surface. Look for them near mountains.

hematite
crystal

CHAPTER 3

What tools do you need?
A hammer. A bucket. A pick.
Wear hiking shoes. Bring water
to drink. And always bring
an adult with you.

Keep your eyes open. You never
know what you might find!

ACTIVITIES & TOOLS

MAKE CRYSTAL CANDY

Watch crystals grow as delicious candy forms.

What You Need:
- 1 cup water
- small pot
- 3 cups sugar
- spoon
- food coloring (optional)
- clean glass jar
- string (not nylon) or yarn
- pencil

❶ **Pour the water in the small pot. With an adult's help, boil the water.**

❷ **Stir in the sugar one spoonful at a time. Make sure it dissolves in the hot water.**

❸ **Add a few drops of food coloring.**

❹ **Ask an adult to help you pour the water from the pot into the glass jar.**

❺ **Tie the string to the pencil.**

❻ **Balance the pencil and string on the jar's opening. The string should hang down into the water. It should not touch the bottom or sides of the jar.**

❼ **Put the jar in a safe place.**

❽ **Check your crystal candy the next day. As the sugar-water cools, crystals should form on the string.**

❾ **When the crystals stop getting bigger, take them out of the jar. Let them dry.**

❿ **Enjoy your crystal candy!**

GLOSSARY

atoms: The smallest building blocks of matter that combine to form molecules.

calcite: A mineral substance made up of calcium carbonate.

cavities: Empty spaces in something solid.

compounds: Combinations of two or more elements.

evaporates: When a liquid changes into vapor or gas.

fault: A large break in Earth's surface that can cause an earthquake.

gypsum: A mineral consisting of hydrous calcium sulfate.

hot springs: Sources of hot water that flow naturally from the ground.

magma: Melted rock beneath Earth's surface that becomes lava when it flows out of volcanoes and fissures.

matter: Something that has weight and takes up space, such as a solid, liquid, or gas.

minerals: Solid, natural substances with crystal structures, usually obtained from the ground.

molecules: Two or more atoms that join together.

quartz: A common mineral consisting of silicon dioxide that is often found in the form of colorless transparent crystals but is sometimes brightly colored.

selenite: The crystal masses of gypsum.

volcano: A mountain with openings through which molten lava, ash, and hot gases erupt.

INDEX

TO LEARN MORE

Learning more is as easy as 1, 2, 3.

1) Go to www.factsurfer.com

2) Enter "crystals" into the search box.

3) Click the "Surf" button to see a list of websites.

With factsurfer, finding more information is just a click away.